ASIAPAC COMIC SERIES

The Message of
the Benevolent

THE SAYINGS OF CONFUCIUS

孔子說

Edited and illustrated by
Tsai Chih Chung

Translated by
Goh Beng Choo

ASIAPAC . SINGAPORE

Publisher
ASIAPAC BOOKS PTE LTD
629 Aljunied Road
#04-06 Cititech Industrial Building
Singapore 1438
Tel: 7453868
Fax: 7453822

First published May 1989
Reprinted Oct 1989, April 1990, Dec 1990
Dec 1991, Jan 1993, Oct 1993

© ASIAPAC BOOKS, 1989
ISBN 9971-985-41-1

Cover design by Soffian
Typeset by Superskill Graphics Pte Ltd
Printed in Singapore by Loi Printing Pte Ltd

Publisher's Note

As a publisher dedicated to the promotion of Chinese culture and literary works, we are pleased to present you the **Chinese Philosophers in Comics** by famous cartoonist Tsai Chih Chung to enable you to understand the schools of thought of the great Chinese ancient sages such as Zhuang Zi, Confucius and Lao Zi.

The Sayings of Confucius features the life of Confucius, selected sayings from *Lun Yu* (The Analects) and some of his more prominent pupils. It enables you to understand Confucius as a person, his philosophy and his teachings. Although meant as a stimulus, it is a must especially for those who wish to understand the humanity and moral values of the Chinese.

We feel honoured to have Tsai Chih Chung's permission to the translation rights to his best-selling comic series and would also like to thank Goh Beng Choo for putting in her best efforts in the translation of this series.

Asiapac's new corporate identity design

The Asiapac Books corporate symbol has its original inspiration from the Chinese character for Asia. The central globe symbolizes the international market for which we publish and distribute books, thereby helping to bridge the East and the West. The open book resembling soaring wings represents Asiapac, ever dynamic and innovative, aiming to communicate with modern society through the printed page. The green colour expresses Asiapac's commitment to go "green for life".

Foreword

Confucius Was Human Too
On the comic book of 'The Sayings of Confucius'

Confucius is the sage of China, and The Analects can be said to be the bible of China. It follows that the preachings of Confucius are a must in my series of Chinese philosophers in comics. In fact, The Analects came out tops in the list of preferred publications named in the letters written by readers to me.

The Analects contains many beautiful phrases which have been widely quoted by people from all quarters through the ages. The preachings of Confucius have, for more than two thousand years, remained universally applicable. A significant one is his view that real knowledge comes from saying what one knows when one knows it and what one does not when one does not know it. It might be possible that, among his pupils, he had singled out Zi Lu to give this advice because Zi Lu was prone to weakness in this area. Yet how often and how common it is today for the people of our time to make the same mistake; people who do not know the truth behind things pretending that they do and even going on to make known their rather ludicrous views on these things!

Confucius was human too, and the most endearing quality of being human must surely be that touch of humanity and the ability to feel sad and happy, sorrowful and angry. Confucius sang when he was happy, showed his anger when he was angry, shed tears when he felt sad and was quick to rebuke and embarrass when things went wrong. He would occasionally crack a joke or two; he was successful in certain things he did, but failed in other things – he was not infallible like the gods. You may find his preachings more approachable if, after reading this book, you come to realise that Confucius was just like you and I.

There is a point which I would like to stress here. Right from the time when I started work on 'The Sayings of Zhuang Zi', I have given consideration to the problems of research. One example is the fact that brush and paper were not invented yet during the Spring and Autumn Period, neither were gold ingots used as money then. But if I were to illustrate the characters writing on bamboo slips (as the Chinese living in that age did), the reader might mistake them to be carving instead of writing. I have therefore decided to use symbols in depicting such things, bearing in mind that the aim of this series is to simplify ancient books rather than to engage in research. I hope you would understand and forgive me on this point.

Tsai Chih Chung
Taiwan

Chinese Philosophers In Comics
The Sayings of Confucius
Edited & Illustrated by Tsai Chih Chung
Translated by Goh Beng Choo

Tsai Chih Chung was born in 1948 in the Chang Hwa County of Taiwan. He began drawing cartoon strips at the age of 17 and worked as Art Director for Kuang Chi Programme Service in 1971. He founded the Far East Animation Production Company and the Dragon Cartoon Production Company in 1976, where he produced two cartoon films entitled 'Old Master Q' and 'Shao Lin Temple'.

Mr Tsai first got his four-box comics published in newspapers and magazines in 1983. His funny comic characters such as the Drunken Swordsman, Fat Dragon, One-eyed Marshal and Bold Supersleuth have been serialised in newspapers in Singapore, Malaysia, Taiwan, Hong Kong, Japan, Europe and the United States.

He was voted one of the Ten Outstanding Young People of Taiwan in 1985 and was acclaimed by the media and the educational circle in Taiwan.

The comic book of 'The Sayings of Zhuang Zi' was published in 1986 and marked a milestone in Tsai's career. Within two years, 'Zhuang Zi' went into more than 70 reprints in Taiwan and 15 in Hong Kong and has to date sold over 175,000 copies. There is also a Japanese translation of the book.

In 1987, Mr Tsai published 'The Sayings of Lao Zi', 'The Sayings of Confucius' and a few books based on Zen and mythology. Since then, he has published 26 titles, out of which 10 are about ancient thinkers and the rest are based on historical and literary classics. All these books topped the bestsellers' list at one time or another. In early 1989, three of these, 'Zhuang Zi', 'Zen Talk' and 'The Sixth Buddhist Master', sold 6,000 copies in Beijing within 3 days.

Mr Tsai can be said to be the pioneer in the art of visualising Chinese literature and philosophy by way of comics.

About the Translator

Goh Beng Choo, a Singaporean, received her BA degree from the University of Singapore (now known as the National University of Singapore).

In 1978, she worked as a freelance stringer for the now defunct New Nation, writing serialised bilingual stories taken from Chinese proverbs.

From 1984 to 1993, Ms Goh was a bilingual journalist with The Straits Times, Singapore's leading newspaper. She was attached to the Bilingual Desk, Section Two of the paper, where she reported and reviewed arts and literary events organised in Singapore, Hong Kong and Taiwan in English and Chinese languages.

At present she works as a freelance bilingual writer and media consultant.

Ms Goh has translated into English 'The Sayings of Zhuang Zi' by Mr Tsai Chih Chung and several poems and short stories written by Chinese-language writer Yeng Pway Ngon. She is also the translator of the Chinese edition of Tan Kok Seng's novel 'Son of Singapore'.

Translator's Note

Unlike 'The Sayings of Zhuang Zi' which appeals to the sense of aesthetics attributed to Zhuang Zi, a naturalist who looked to nature for inspiration, this collection of Confucius' sayings and the story of his life rivets with elements of human interest. Many of the sage's ideas are relevant to modern-day living and are therefore well worth a thought.

In this edition, Confucius and his disciples are enlivened by Tsai Chih Chung's vivid drawings of rich facial expressions. These figures, created sensitively, do give the moralistic messages a sugar-coating effect and humanise the image of these great men, particularly that of Confucius himself.

This comics book not only captures the warm relationship between the sage and his disciples through records of simple, everyday encounters, but also offers food for thought for the modern man and woman who are searching for guidance in the course of self-development.

There are two favourite sayings of mine among the many inspirational reflections contained in this book. One is, "Do not worry that you are not discovered, ask yourself what it is you have that is worthy of people's recognition"; and the other, the view that knowledge means to "say you know when you know" and to "say you do not when you do not."

As citizens of an efficient country who might be inclined towards complacency because of the many achievements we have made, a sense of humility is certainly well cultivating in this competitive, fast-changing world where no nation can stay on top indefinitely.

In translating Mr Tsai's book, I have referred to Dr D.C. Lau's English translation entitled 'Confucius The Analects' published in Penguin Classics. This book is recommended for readers who wish to read The Analects in full with an introduction given by Dr Lau.

Contents

The Life
of
Confucius

Kong Qiu, also Kong Zhongni, was born around
551 B.C. He is more commonly known as Confucius.

1

The Life of Confucius

Confucius was born in the Chang Ping Village of the state of Lu, during King Ling of Zhou's twenty-first year in reign (BC 551).

YAN

QI

○ LU

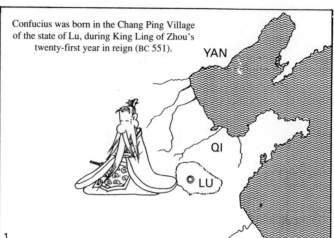

1

Confucius' father was Kong Shu Liang He, a mighty man of ten *chi* tall. He had nine daughters by his wife and a son by his concubine, but the boy was unfortunately handicapped.

2

After the age of sixty-four, Shu Liang He married Madam Yuan, who bore him Confucius.

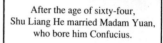

3

When Confucius was three, his father passed away.

As a child, Confucius loved to lay out the different sacrificial vessels at play,

5

During which he would imitate the rituals and gestures of adults at ceremonies.

6

2

When Confucius was fifteen, his mind became fixed on learning.

At the age of nineteen, he married Yuan Guan from the state of Song.

The following year, they had a son and named him Kong Li, meaning 'carp'.

At the age of twenty, Confucius worked as a clerk at the granaries,

Where he was noted for his accuracy and preciseness in keeping accounts.

Later he was made overseer of the flocks and grazing grounds. The flocks were so well tended that they flourished.

Years later, he worked as a foreman of building constructions.

3

30 During the Spring and Autumn Period, the states were in shambles. The rulers did not behave like rulers and subjects did not behave like subjects.

Duke Zhao was eventually defeated and expelled by Ji Sun.

31 And Duke Jing of Qi was under the control of Chen Heng, who was so powerful that it seemed he could usurp Duke Jing's position any time.

So, when Duke Jing asked Confucius about the formula for good government, Confucius answered:

32 Let the ruler be like a ruler, the subject be like a subject, the father be like a father, and the son be like a son.

33 Right, if people do not behave in the manners befitting their positions, even if there is grain, would we get to eat it in peace?

What is the principle of governing then?

The most important thing about governing is to use your resources wisely and curb your excesses.

34

35 I want to give my land at Ni Xi to Confucius.

7

Duke Zhao was forced into exile and wandered for seven years. He died outside his state and Duke Ding succeeded the throne.

42

But Duke Ding was powerless and the state was controlled by the three families of Ji, Shu and Meng.

43

Ji Sun, who was at the helm in Lu, was in turn terrorised into obedience by Yang Huo, a steward of his house.

44

In the fifth year of the reign of Duke Ding, Yang Huo staged a revolt and seized power from Ji Sun.

45

He terrorised Duke Ding into obedience, sent his opponents into exile and became dictator of Lu.

46

With no desire to serve a government which violated the rites, Confucius retired to concentrate on the study of *Shu* (History), *Shi* (The Odes), *Li* (Rites) and *Yue* (Music).

47

9

In the eighth year of Duke Ding's reign, Yang Huo decided to remove the three families from power.

Destroy the three families! I shall replace them!.

Yes, Your Highness!

55

56 The three families fought tooth-and-nail to safeguard their power.

57

Yang Huo was defeated by them and he fled to Qi.

Yang Huo's failure gave Confucius an opportunity to take part in governmental affairs.

58

59 Ji Sun admired Confucius greatly for not pandering to Yang Huo. He recommended Confucius to Duke Ding of Lu.

60 Duke Ding made Confucius governor of the middle district of Lu.

61 Confucius, who was in office for only a year, was so efficient that officials of the neighbouring estates modelled their policies after his.

62 Confucius was further promoted to the rank of Minister of Public Works and then to that of Police Commissioner to keep law and peace.

63 During those years, the criminals and illegal traders of Lu either turned over a new leaf or left the state on their own.

64 Because Confucius moved the people with virtue and educated them with rites, everyone in Lu respected the elderly;

65 The men and women of Lu walked at a distance from each other. Things left behind by owners were never picked up and at night, doors were left unlocked without fear of robbery.

15

17

93
Execute them!

94 Duke Jing was moved by the stern countenance of Confucius.

95 After returning to Qi, he felt uneasy.

The Prince of Lu is assisted by the rites of the gentleman, while you guys peddled to me the ways of the barbarian. What shall I do?

96 If a gentleman made a mistake, he apologises with action. A petty man apologises with words. Maybe fulfilling the pact may put Your Majesty at ease.

97 Alright. I shall return the occupied lands to Lu as a token of apology.

Yes, Your Majesty.

109 They finally succeeded in tearing down the city of Fei.

110 Now get ready to tear down the city of Cheng!

Yes, Your Majesty.

111 But Lord Lian Chu of the Cheng City said to Meng Sun:

Once Cheng City is torn down, the Qi soldiers are sure to press in on us from the north.

112 Do not forget that Cheng City is a fortification for the Meng family. There can be no Meng family without Cheng City and I am quite prepared to defy your command.

113 In the twelfth month, Duke Ding besieged Cheng City but failed to conquer it.

21

114 In Duke Ding's thirteenth year, Confucius took part in the government in the capacity of Minister of Justice. Happiness was written all over his face.

115 We have heard it said that a gentleman shows no fear in bad times, neither does he jump for joy in good times.

116 Yes, that has been said. Still, there is no harm in a gentleman taking delight in himself among his friends.

117 And he proceeded to have Shao Zheng Mao — the Counsellor who created political trouble for Lu — executed.

118 Confucius was only in government for three months, and the pork-sellers and lamb-sellers all stopped falsifying their prices.

Fixed Price

People from the west who visited Lu were warmly received and spared the need to apply for entry permit.

LU STATE

No entry permit is required for visitors.

119

120

Duke Jing of Qi got worried upon news about the smooth running of Lu.

If Confucius continues to be in charge, Lu will become the supreme state. Since we are the nearest to them, our land will be the first to be annexed.

Let's sabotage their reforms and pick some beauties for Prince Lu.

121

122

Yes, that's a good idea.

123

So Qi presented eighty beauties and one hundred and twenty horses to the Prince of Lu.

124

Duke Jing has sent us beauties and horses. They are stationed at the High Gate on the south.

125

Let's have a look at them.

Since then, Duke Ding and Ji Sun indulged themselves in pleasure-seeking and did not attend to official duties for three days.

126

At the sacrificial feast, they did not give the counsellors sacrificial meat in accordance with the rites.

127

Let's leave this place.

Yes, let's go.

128

Now that Yang Huo's supporters have been wiped out, Ji Sun's position is stable, I wouldn't be of any use any more. Besides, the prince has no real power... Let's go.

129

130

Thereafter Confucius resigned and left Lu to go to Wei.

24

131 When Confucius arrived in Wei, he was impressed by the flourishing population of the state.

132 What a flourishing population!

What must be done after the population has flourished?

Make the people rich.

133

134 What must be done after making them rich?

Educate them.

135 Confucius put up with Yan Zhuo Zou, Zi Lu's brother-in-law.

27

29

192 On one occasion, Duke Ling asked Confucius about military tactics...

193 I know something about sacrificial rites, but nothing about military affairs.

194 The following day, while Duke Ling and Confucius were having a conversation, a flight of wild geese flew past and caught the glance of the Duke, who paid no attention to what Confucius was saying.

195 The Master decided to leave Wei to go to Chen.

196 The next year he went from Chen to Cai.

37

Confucius turned sixty-eight in the eleventh year of the reign of Duke Ai and Ji Kang Zi set off to welcome him back to Lu with pompous ceremony.

208

It had been fourteen years since Confucius left Lu to travel among the states.

209

Although Duke Ai and Ji Kang Shi did seek Confucius' advice on government matters, the Master's ideas were never put to use.

210

211

No longer hoping for an official post, Confucius stayed home a good deal of time to edit The Odes (*Shi Jing*), compile the ancient music and rites, preserve the *I Ching* and edit the Spring and Autumn Annals.

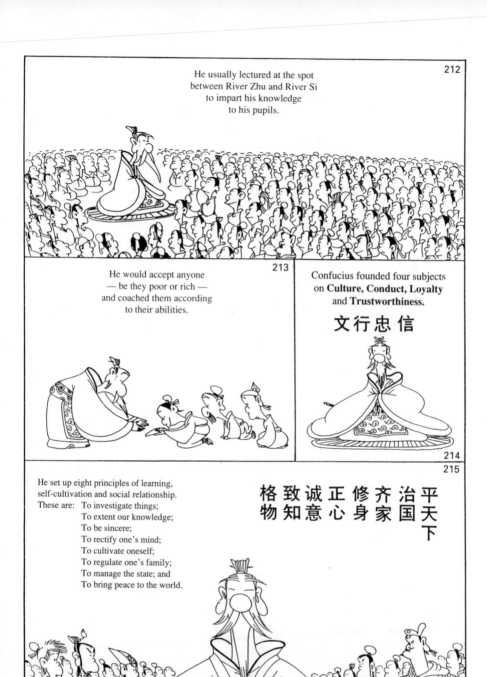

212

He usually lectured at the spot
between River Zhu and River Si
to impart his knowledge
to his pupils.

213

He would accept anyone
— be they poor or rich —
and coached them according
to their abilities.

Confucius founded four subjects
on **Culture, Conduct, Loyalty**
and **Trustworthiness.**

文 行 忠 信

214

215

He set up eight principles of learning,
self-cultivation and social relationship.

These are:　To investigate things;
　　　　　　To extent our knowledge;
　　　　　　To be sincere;
　　　　　　To rectify one's mind;
　　　　　　To cultivate oneself;
　　　　　　To regulate one's family;
　　　　　　To manage the state; and
　　　　　　To bring peace to the world.

格 致 诚 正 修 齐 治 平
物 知 意 心 身 家 国 天
　　　　　　　　　下

216

Thereafter one should proceed to learn the Rites, Music, Archery, Horsemanship, History and Mathematics, to reach the three virtues of **Wisdom**, **Benevolence** and **Courage**.

217

Confucius divided his teachings into four stages:
to set one's mind on the Way;
to base oneself on virtue;
to rely on benevolence for
    support; and
to seek recreation in the arts.

志　据　依　游
于　于　于　于
道　德　仁　艺

Literature

Government

On his list of priorities, **Conduct** is the first requirement, **Speech** comes second, **Government Matters** third and **Literature** last.

Language

Virtue

218

224 Seven days later, Confucius passed away.

225 He died in the fourth lunar month in the sixteenth year of Duke Ai, at the age of seventy-three.

226

The historian Si Ma Qian said:

These lines appear in The Odes:
Majestic indeed is the mountain that we look up to;
Great indeed is the virtue that we seek to emulate.

As a commoner, Confucius' teachings were sustained for more than a thousand years. There is no intellectual who does not regard him as his spiritual mentor. Confucius is indeed the supreme sage!

43

论　语

LUN YU - The Analects

Chapter 1, paragraph 1,
To Learn

学而时习之，不亦说乎？
有朋自远方来，不亦乐乎？
人不知而不愠，不亦君子乎？

学而第一——

Isn't it a joy to acquire knowledge and be able to put it to use?

1

Isn't it a great pleasure to have a friend visiting from afar?

2

Isn't he a gentleman who bears no grudge against those who do not know his strength?

3

45

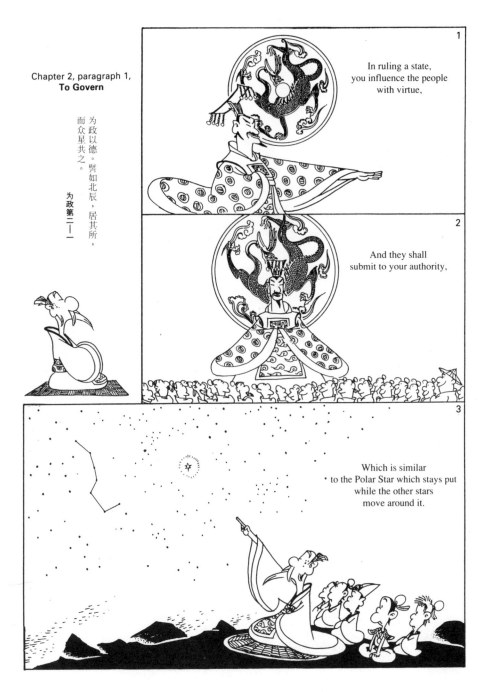

Chapter 2, paragraph 1,
To Govern

为政以德。譬如北辰，居其所，而众星共之。

为政第二—一

1 In ruling a state,
you influence the people
with virtue,

2 And they shall
submit to your authority,

3 Which is similar
to the Polar Star which stays put
while the other stars
move around it.

47

Chapter 2, paragraph 4,
To Govern

吾十有五而志于学；
三十而立；
四十而不惑；
五十而知天命；六十而耳顺；
七十而从心所欲，不踰矩。

为政第二—四

1 When I was fifteen, I set my mind on learning,

2 At thirty, I held on firmly to what I've learned.

3 At forty, I knew all about managing affairs and understanding truth.

4 At fifty, I realised that Heaven had its own will. I blamed neither Heaven nor man.

5 At sixty, I could tell whether a man was telling the truth and judge his character by listening to his speech.

6 At seventy, I could follow my heart's wishes and not make mistakes.

48

Chapter 2, paragraph 17,
To Govern

子曰：
「由，誨女，知之乎？
知之為知之，
不知為不知，
是知也。」

為政第二十七

49

子入大廟，每事問。
或曰：「孰謂鄹人之
子知禮乎？入大廟，
每事問。」
子聞之曰：「是禮也！」

八佾第三—十五

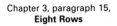

When Confucius first entered the temple of the Duke of Zhou to assist with making sacrifices, he asked questions about everything.

Who said that the son of the man from Zhou knows about rites? He asks questions about everything in the temple.

To ask questions about everything in a modest manner is to know the proper rite.

50

Chapter 3, paragraph 17,
Eight Rows

子貢欲去告朔之餼羊。
子曰：「賜也！爾愛其羊，
我愛其禮。」
八佾第三—十七

Chapter 4, paragraph 9,
To Live Among the Benevolent

Chapter 4, paragraph 14,
**To Live Among
the Benevolent**

不患无位，患所以立。
不患莫己知，求为可知也。
里仁第四—十四。

Do not worry that
you have no position,

Worry that you may not
have the necessary
qualifications.

1

2

3

Do not worry
that you are not being
discovered.

Ask yourself what it
is you have that is worthy of
people's recognition.

4

53

Chapter 4, paragraph 17,
To Live Among the Benevolent

见贤思齐焉，见不贤而
内自省也。
里仁第四—十七

1

When I meet an able and virtuous man, I aim at being his equal.

2

When I meet a man who is neither able nor virtuous,

wine

3

I engage in self-reflection,

4

wine

To see if I share his undesirable traits in any way.

54

Chapter 4, paragraph 19,
To Live Among the Benevolent

父母在，不遠遊；
游必有方。
里仁第四—十九

When your parents are alive, you should not travel far;

If you must do so, you should always tell them your whereabouts to save them the anguish of worrying for you.

德不孤，必有邻。
里仁第四—二五

1

A virtuous man is never lonely.

2

Others who are as virtuous as he is
are bound to be drawn to him.

Chapter 5, paragraph 9,
Gong Ye Zhang

Chapter 5, paragraph 14,
Gong Ye Zhang

子貢問曰：「孔
文子何以謂之文
也？」子曰：「敏
而好學，不恥下
問，是以謂之文
也。」

公冶長第五—十四

Chapter 5, paragraph 24,
Gong Ye Zhang

巧言、令色、足恭，左丘明恥之，丘亦恥之。匿怨而友其人，左丘明恥之，丘亦恥之。

公冶長第五－二四

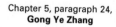

1
To utter sweet words,
display ingratiating manners
and be overly humble.

2
These are conducts
Zuo Qiu Ming considered
shameful. I, too, find
them shameful.

3
To bear hatred towards someone
while being superficially friendly.

4
This Zuo Qiu Ming
found shameful. I, too,
find it shameful.

60

Chapter 5, paragraph 25,
Gong Ye Zhang

Chapter 5, paragraph 27,
Gong Ye Zhang

十室之邑，必有忠信如丘者焉，
不如丘之好學也。

公冶長第五—二七

Within the hamlet of
only ten families,

It is not difficult to find
someone as conscientious
and trustworthy as I,

But only that he
may not possess as much
love for learning.

63

Chapter 6, paragraph 9,
Ran Yong

述而不作，
信而好古，
竊比于我老彭。
述而第七一一。

I transmit but do not create,

I believe firmly in
the ways of the ancient kings
and have a love for
the ancient culture.

I emulate the fine example
of Old Peng of the
Shang Dynasty.

Chapter 7, paragraph 2,
To Transmit

默而識之，學而不厭，誨人不倦；
何有于我哉？

述而第七—二

1 Memorising the knowledge
I have learned deeply.

Not feeling tired
of learning,

2

3 Not growing weary in teaching,

4 All these come easy to me.

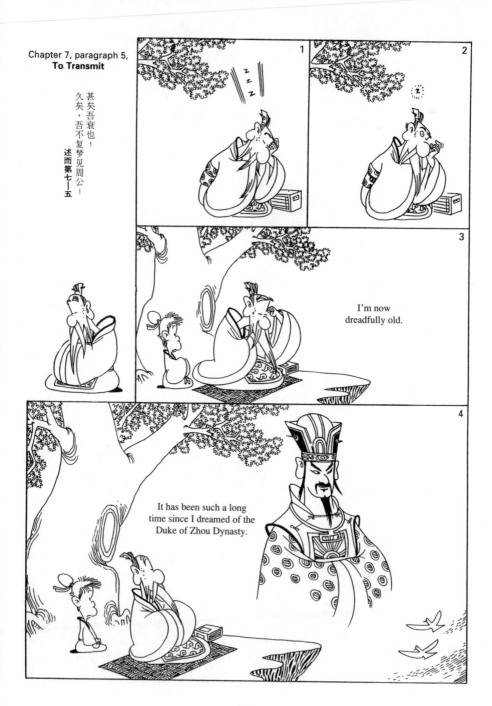

Chapter 7, paragraph 6,
To Transmit

志於道，據於德，依於仁，游於藝。

述而第七—六

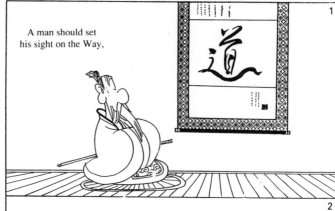

A man should set
his sight on the Way,

1

Base his conduct
on virtue,

德

2

3

Be guided by benevolence
in living and finally,

4

Take recreation
in the arts.

69

Chapter 7, paragraph 7,
To Transmit

自行束脩以上，
吾未尝无诲焉！

述而第七—七

To anyone who offers any gift
in respect of the teacher,

I'm only too glad to
receive him and coach him.

Chapter 7, paragraph 8,
To Transmit

不愤，不启；
不悱，不发。
举一隅不
以三隅反，
则不复也。

述而第七—八

1 I never enlighten anyone who is never driven to frustration by the urge to seek knowledge.

2 Nor do I illuminate anyone who is never driven to frenzy by the urge to seek knowledge.

3 When I have pointed out one corner of a square to him,

And he cannot make the connection with the other three, I will not teach him again.

4

Chapter 7, paragraph 19,
To Transmit

我非生而知之者；好古，敏以求之者也。

述而第七—十九

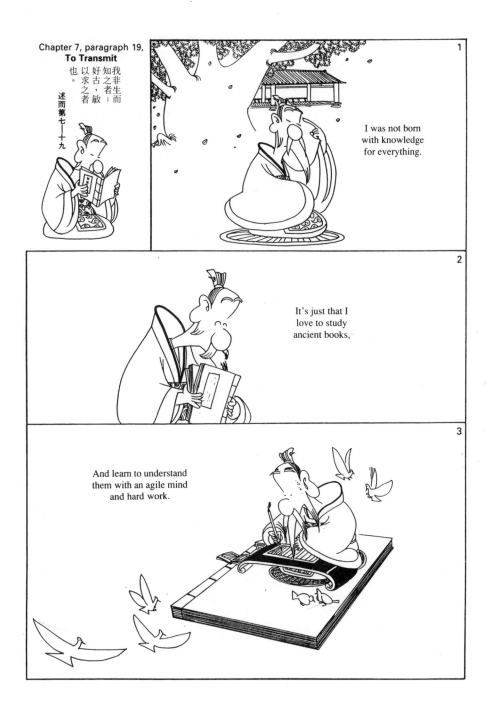

三人行，必有我師焉。擇其善
者而從之；其不善者而改之。
述而第七—二一

When I'm walking in the company of two other men, there is always something I can learn from them...

1

Their strengths I pick up.

2

Their weaknesses I use for self-correction.

wine

3

74

Chapter 7, paragraph 26,
To Transmit

子釣而不綱；

弋不射宿。

述而第七─二六

The Master fishes with a fishing rod,

But not with a large net.

He shoots with arrows,

But never shoots
at roosting birds.

1

2

3

4

75

Chapter 8, paragraph 4,
Count Tai

曾子有疾，孟敬子問之。
曾子言曰：「鳥之將死，
其鳴也哀；人之將死，其言也善。
君子所貴乎道者三：動容貌，
暴慢矣；正顏色，斯近信矣；
出辭氣，斯遠鄙倍矣。
籩豆之事，則有司存。」

泰伯第八—四

1
When Zeng Zi was ill,
Meng Jing Zi came to see him.
Zeng Zi said:

Wa!

Sad is the cry
of a dying bird;

2
Kind are the words
of a dying man.

3
There are three
things in the Way
which a gentleman
values most:

4
To maintain a polite countenance in order to stay
away from the boorish;
to keep an honest expression in order to gain trust;
to talk reasonably in order to avoid being senseless.

As for sacrificial rites, there are officials responsible
for them.

76

Chapter 8, paragraph 17,
Count Tai

学如不及，
犹恐失之。
泰伯第八—十七

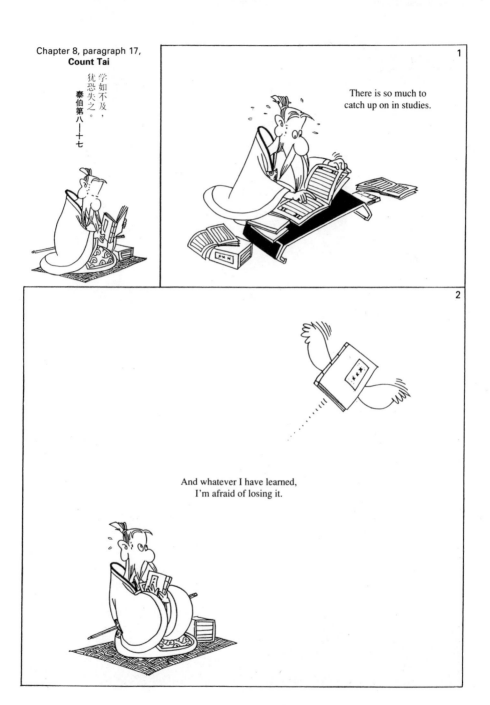

1

There is so much to
catch up on in studies.

2

And whatever I have learned,
I'm afraid of losing it.

Chapter 9, paragraph 16,
Rarely Does the Master

逝者如斯夫！
不舍晝夜。
子罕第九—十六

Is this how everything
in life passes?

Day and night without a break.

Chapter 9, paragraph 28,
**Rarely Does
the Master...**

知者不惑，仁者不忧，
勇者不惧。
子罕第九—二八

1

The wise is
never confused.

2

The benevolent
is never worried.

3

The courageous is never afraid.

Chapter 10, paragraph 11,
At Home

廐焚。子退朝，
曰：「傷人乎？」
不問馬。

鄉黨第十一

Confucius' stables caught fire.

On returning from court, he asked:

Was anyone hurt?

He did not ask if the horses were hurt.

Chapter 11, paragraph 11,
The Pioneers

季路問事鬼神？
子曰：「未能事人，
焉能事鬼？」
曰：「敢問死？」
曰：「未知生，焉知死？」
先進第十一·十一

1. Zi Lu asked about the way to serve the spirits of the dead and the gods.

2. You don't even know how to serve man, how can you serve the dead?

3. May I ask about death?

4. You don't even understand life, how can you understand death?

Chapter 11, paragraph 15,
The Pioneers

子貢問：「師與商也孰賢？」
子曰：「師也過，商也
不及。」
曰：「然則師愈與？」
子曰：「過猶不及。」
先進第十一—十五

1 Who is superior? Zi Zhang or Zi Xia?

Zi Gong asked:

2 Zi Zhang overshoots the mark;

3 Zi Xia falls slightly short.

4 Does that mean Zi Zhang is superior?

5 Overshooting is as undesirable as falling short.

83

Chapter 11, paragraph 17,
The Pioneers

柴也愚，參也魯，師也辟，由也喭。
回也其庶乎！屢空。賜不受命而貨
殖焉，億則屢中。

先進第十一—十七

1
Gao Chai is dull-witted.

2
Zeng Shen is slow.

3
Chuan Sun Shi is extroverted and lacks honesty.

4
Zhong You is aggressive.

5
Yan Hui has inclinations for scholarly achievement but his ambitions are often trapped by poverty!

6
Duan Mu Ci refuses to accept his lot and went into business. His speculations on prices are so accurate that he makes huge profits.

Chapter 12, paragraph 1,
Yan Hui

颜渊问仁。子曰：「克己复礼为仁。
一日克己复礼，天下归仁焉。
为仁由己，而由人乎哉？」
颜渊曰：「请问其目？」
子曰：「非礼勿视，非礼勿听、
非礼勿言，非礼勿动。」
颜渊曰：「回虽不敏，
请事斯语矣！」
颜渊第十二—一

Chapter 12, paragraph 16,
Yan Hui

君子成人之美，不成
人之惡；小人反是。

顏淵第十二—十六

He is a nice man;
go and serve him.

This man is
excellent; it would
do you good to
employ him.

The gentleman helps others
to utilise their strengths
and not their weaknesses;

This man is
wicked; you'd
better not work
for him.

This man
is lousy;
you mustn't
employ him.

The small man
does the opposite.

Chapter 12, paragraph 24,
Yan Hui

曾子曰：「君子以文会友；
以友辅仁。」
颜渊第十二──二四

1

Zeng Zi said:

A gentleman makes friends
through being cultured,

2

And looks to friends
to help him cultivate
benevolence.

Chapter 13, paragraph 13,
Zi Lu

苟正其身矣，于从政乎何有？
不能正其身，如正人何？

子路第十三—十三

Chapter 13, paragraph 17,
Zi Lu

子夏为莒父宰，问政。
子曰：「无欲速，无见
小利；欲速则不达，
见小利则大事不成。」

子路第十三—十七

Zi Xia became prefect
of Ju Fu.

He sought advice
from Confucius
on government.

Do not hope for quick
results; do not see just
petty gains.

If you want quick
results, you can never
complete your tasks.

And if you only see
petty gains, you can never
achieve great things.

91

Chapter 14, paragraph 13,
Xian Enquires

子路問成人。
子曰：「若臧武仲之知，
公綽之不欲，卞莊子之勇，
冉求之藝；文之以禮樂，
亦可為成人矣！」
曰：「今之成人者，何必然？
見利思義，見危授命，
久要不忘平生之言，
亦可以為成人矣！」
憲問第十四—十三

1 Zi Lu asked: What makes a complete man?

2 A man as intelligent as Zang Wu Zhong,

3 As free from greed as Meng Gong Chuo,

4 As courageous as Zhuang Zi of Bian,

5 As talented as Ran Qiu and is well-versed in the rites and music. These qualities make a complete man.

6 But nowadays to be a complete man, one need not have all these qualities. If you remember what is right at the sight of benefit, is ready to die in times of danger and never forget to keep old promises, you may be considered a complete man.

其言之不怍，

则为之也难！

宪问第十四—二一

For a man to have nothing
to be ashamed of and
nothing to hide,

1

It means putting
his daily conduct to severe tests.

2

94

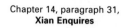

Chapter 14, paragraph 31,
Xian Enquires

子貢方人。
子曰：「賜也，
賢乎哉？夫我
則不暇！」
憲問第十四—三一

Zi Gong loves
to criticise people.

Ha! Ha! Ha!

1

Are you yourself
a perfect man,
Duan Mu Ci?

!

2

As for me,
I really have no time
to criticise others!

3

骥
不
称
其
力
，
称
其
德
。

宪问第十四—三五

1

A good horse is
praised not for
its power,

2

But for its tameness.

Chapter 14, paragraph 36,
Xian Enquires

或曰：「以德報怨，何如？」
子曰：「何以報德？
以直報怨，以德報德。」
憲問第十四—三六

1 Someone once
asked Confucius:

What do you say
if I repay an injury
with a favour?

2 What do you
repay a favour with?

3 You repay an injury
with impartiality;

4 And a favour
with a favour.

98

Chapter 14, paragraph 37,
Xian Enquires

子曰：「莫我知也夫！」
子貢曰：「何為其莫知子也？」
子曰：「不怨天，不尤人，下學而上達：
知我者，其天乎！」
憲問第十四—三七

子路宿于石門。
晨門曰：「奚自？」
子路曰：「自孔氏。」
曰：「是知其不可而為
之者與？」

憲問第十四—四一

100

Chapter 14, paragraph 46,
Xian Enquires

原壤夷俟。子曰：
「幼而不孫弟，
長而無述焉，
老而不死
是為賊！」
以杖叩其脛。
憲問第十四—四六

1

When Yuan Rang, Confucius'
old friend saw him coming,
he squatted down on the ground
to wait for him.

2 When you were young,
you were neither
modest nor
filial.

3 When you grew up,
you did nothing
worthwhile,

4 And now you are
old, you refuse to
die. You are a
pest indeed!

5 So said, the Master tapped
him on the shin with a
walking stick.

TAP! TAP!

Chapter 15, paragraph 6,
Duke Ling of Wei

直哉史鱼！邦有道，如矢；邦无道，如矢。君子哉蘧伯玉！邦有道，则仕；邦无道，则可卷而怀之。

卫灵公第十五——六

1

What an upright character Shi Yu is! When the state is run orderly, he serves it loyally and is as straight as an arrow;

2

When the state is in disarray, he offers frank advice and is still as straight as an arrow.

3

What a gentleman Qu Po Yu is! When the state is run orderly, he takes office,

4

When the state is in disarray, he retreats, withholding his talent.

102

子貢問仁。子曰：「工欲
善其事，必先利其器。居是
邦也，事其大夫之賢者，友
其士之仁者。」

卫灵公第十五—九

1

If the craftsman wants to do a good job, he must first sharpen his tools.

Zi Gong asked about the cultivation of benevolence.

2

In whatever state you live, you should work for a capable government,

3

And make friends with benevolent gentlemen.

Chapter 15, paragraph 11,
Duke Ling of Wei

人无远虑，
必有近忧。
卫灵公第十五—十一

1

A man who does not think far ahead in whatever he does,

2

Is sure to be troubled by worries much closer at hand.

104

Chapter 15, paragraph 23,
Duke Ling of Wei

子貢問曰：「有一言而可以終身行之者乎？」
子曰：「其恕乎！己所不欲，勿施于人。」
卫灵公第十五－二三

* forbearance

105

Chapter 15, paragraph 30,
Duke Ling of Wei

吾嘗終日不食，終夜不寢，以思；無益，不如學也。

卫灵公第十五—三十

1

I have tried to go without food for the whole day,

2

And without sleep for the whole night.

3

Pondering hard, but to no avail.

4

I realise it's more practical to engage in learning.

Chapter 16, paragraph 7,
Ji Family

君子有三戒：
少之時，血氣未定
，戒之在色；及其
壯也，血氣方剛
，戒之在鬥；及
其老也，血氣既
衰，戒之在得。

季氏第十六―七

There are three things
that the gentleman
should guard against:
When he is young,
his blood and *qi* * are
unstable, he must
guard against sexual
desires.

1

In his prime, his blood and *qi* are
at their peak, he must guard
against bellicosity.**

2

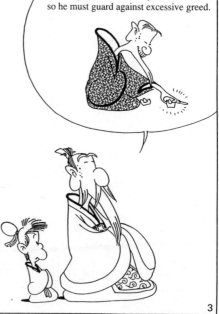

At old age, his blood and *qi* have declined,
so he must guard against excessive greed.

3

* the basic component of the universe. It fills the human body and circulates with the blood.   ** to be war-like by nature

Chapter 16, paragraph 10,
Ji Family

君子有九思：
視思明，聽思聰，
色思溫，貌思恭，
言思忠，事思敬，
疑思問，忿思難，
見得思義。

季氏第十六—十

1 There are nine things which the gentleman should ponder upon:

2 When looking, he must think of seeing clearly.

3 When hearing, he must think of hearing clearly.

4 When expressing his moods, he must look amicable,

5 Behaving in a courteous manner.

6 Honesty... When speaking, he must think of honesty.

7 When working, he must think of giving his best.

8 When in doubt, he must think of questioning.

9 When showing his anger, he must think of the consequences.

10 When he sees a benefit, he must ponder whether he deserves it.

诚不以富，亦祇以异。
齐景公有马千驷，
死之日，民无德而称焉。
伯夷、叔齐饿于首阳之下，
民到于今称之，
其斯之谓与？
季氏第十六—十二

1

The Odes (*Shi Jing*) says that a man should be praised not because of his wealth but because of his superior conduct.

2

Duke Jing of Qi owned 4 000 horses but when he died, the people found nothing praiseworthy about him.

3

Although Bo Yi and Shu Qi starved to death at the foot of Mount Shou Yang, to this day, people are still praising them. That must be what The Odes are referring to.

Chapter 17, paragraph 2,
Yang Huo

性相近也，
習相遠也。
陽貨第十七—二

All men are alike by nature.

But because of differences in education and environment,

Their differences become more and more apparent.

子曰：「由也，女聞六言六蔽矣乎？」
对曰：「未也。」「居！吾語女：
好仁不好学，其蔽也愚；
好知不好学，其蔽也荡；
好信不好学，其蔽也贼；
好直不好学，其蔽也绞；
好勇不好学，其蔽也乱；
好刚不好学，其蔽也狂。」

阳货第十七——八

Chapter 17, paragraph 22,
Yang Huo

饱食终日，无所用心：难矣哉！
不有博弈者乎？为之犹贤乎已！
阳货第十七—二二

A man who idles around
after he has filled his stomach,

Will not have
any achievement at all,

Aren't there such games as the
board game and *Wei Qi**?
Even having a go at them is
better than doing nothing
the whole day.

* a kind of Chinese chess

115

Chapter 17, paragraph 25,
Yang Huo

阳货第十七—二五

唯女子与小人为难养也。近之则不逊，远之则怨。

1
The maids and servants of the household are the most difficult to handle.

2
If you get too close to them, they become insolent.

3
Go away! How rude you are!

4
Huh! Our master looks down on us servants.

If you keep a distance, they will complain.

116

Chapter 17, paragraph 26,
Yang Huo

年四十而見惡焉，
其終也已！
陽貨第十七—二六

Chapter 18, paragraph 1,
The Viscount of Wei

孔子曰：「殷有三仁焉！」
微子去之，
箕子為之奴，
比干諫而死。
微子第十八—一

118

Chapter 18, paragraph 5,
The Viscount of Wei

楚狂接輿，歌而過孔子，曰：
「鳳兮！鳳兮！何德之衰？
往者不可諫，來者猶可追。
已而！已而！今之從政者殆而！」
孔子下，欲與之言；趨而辟之，
不得與之言。

微子第十八－五

Jie Yu, the lunatic of Chu,
passed by Confucius'
chariot, singing:

Phoenix, oh phoenix!
How thy virtue has decayed!
What is past is beyond redemption,
What is to come is not yet gone.

Let it be! Let it be!
Perilous is the fate of those
in government!

Confucius got off his chariot
to talk to him; but he was gone in
a flash and there was no chance
for a discussion.

长沮、桀溺耦而耕。孔子过之，
使子路问津焉。
长沮曰：「夫执舆者为谁？」
子路曰：「为孔丘。」
曰：「是鲁孔丘与？」
曰：「是也。」
曰：「是知津矣！」
问于桀溺，桀溺曰：「子为谁？」
曰：「为仲由。」
曰：「是鲁孔丘之徒与？」
对曰：「然。」
曰：「滔滔者，天下皆是也，
而谁以易之？且而与其从辟人
之士也，岂若从辟世之士哉？」
耰而不辍。
子路行以告。夫子怃然曰：
「鸟兽不可与同群，吾非斯人
之徒与而谁与？天下有道，
丘不与易也。」

微子第十八－六

1　Chang Ju and Jie Ni were ploughing in the field when Confucius passed by in his chariot.

Go and ask them where the ford is.

Yes, Master.

2　Can you please tell me where the ford is?

3　Who's the man holding the reins?

120

121

122

Chapter 19, paragraph 9,
Zi Zhang

子夏曰：「君子有三變：
望之儼然，即之也溫，
聽其言也厲。」
子張第十九—九

Zi Xia said:

"A gentleman always gives others three different impressions: From afar, he appears stately,

On a closer look,
he appears amiable,

But when he speaks,
he sounds stern."

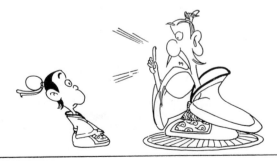

Chapter 19, paragraph 21,
Zi Zhang

子貢曰：「君子之过也，
如日月之食焉；过也，
人皆见之；更也，人皆仰之。」

子张第十九—二一

Zi Gong said:
The gentleman's errors are
like an eclipse of the sun
and moon; when he errs,
the whole world can see it.

When he corrects himself,
the whole world
looks up to him.

Chapter 20, paragraph 3,
Yao Speaks

不知命，无以为
君子也；不知礼，
无以立也；不知言，
无以知人也。
尧曰第二十三

A man who does not know
the will of Heaven cannot
be a gentleman;

A man who knows nothing
about the rites cannot establish
himself in society.

A man who cannot tell right
from wrong is unable to
tell good men from the evil.

Confucius' Pupils

128

Yan Hui 颜回

Yan Hui styled himself Zi Yuan.
He was a native of Lu and was younger
than Confucius by thirty years.

129

Min Sun　闵损

Min Sun styled himself Zi Qian.
He was a native of Lu and was younger
than Confucius by fifteen years.

1

Confucius once praised him.

"What a filial son Min Zi Qian
is. He serves and obeys
his parents and loves his brothers.

2

So much so that there
is no way anyone can
reproach him in front of
his parents and brothers."

3

A man of principle, he once
declined an offer by the
powerful Ji family to be their
steward and would not accept
employment from corrupted
princes. To the messenger
sent by the Ji family, he said:

4

If anyone comes to ask
for me again, tell them
I shall be on the other side
of the River Wen.

Ran Yong 冉雍

Ran Yong styled himself Zhong Gong.
He was a native of Lu and was younger
than Confucius by twenty-nine years.
He came from a poor family for his
father belonged to the lowest
rung of society.

Zhong You　仲由

Zhong You, styled Zi Lu, was a native
of Bian and was younger than Confucius
by nine years. He used to be a boorish,
hearty man who loved muscles and
might, but eventually mellowed through
the influence of Confucius.
In his old age, Zi Lu served as
Counsellor of Pu of Wei.
He was killed in a revolt in Wei.

In learning, Zhong You
has certainly reached the
grand hall of enlightenment,
only that he hasn't quite
penetrated the depths of
the inner chambers yet.

Who else but Zhong You can
stand beside a man garbed in fur
coat, himself in old robes, without
feeling embarrassed?

1

2

Zai Yu　宰予

Zai Yu styled himself Zi Wo. A native of Lu, Zai Yu was an eloquent man well-versed in the art of debate. He was Counsellor of Lin Zi of Qi and was involved in a revolt staged by Tian Chang. Because of him, his whole family was implicated and killed, leaving Confucius to lament deeply for him.

1

Help! Help!

Should a virtuous man jump into the well to rescue a life, the minute he is told that someone has fallen into it?

2

Why must he do that? A gentleman should try to rescue a life by the side of the well, but certainly not to jump into it.

3

A gentleman may be cheated, but he is never ignorant.

Duan Mu Ci
端木賜

Duan Mu Ci, styled Zi Gong, was a native of Wei and was younger than Confucius by thirty-one years. He was eloquent and a good debater who loved to spread the faults as much as the strengths of others.

On more than one occasion, he had helped Lu and Wei out of dire straits. He was wealthy and possessed a business acumen, which earned him fortunes. He died of old age in Qi.

1
What do you think of me, Master?

Zi Gong once asked.

2
You are like a useful vessel.

3
What kind of vessel?

The precious sacrificial vessels that we use in ancestral temples.

4

Bu Shang
卜商

Bu Shang, styled Zi Xia, was a native of Wen and was younger than Confucius by forty-five years.

After the Master had passed away, Zi Xia went and settled in Xi He of Wei, where he recruited pupils and became a teacher of Duke Wen of Wei. When his son died, he cried so hard that he became blind.

1

Zi Xia asked:

The Odes says:
*"Her delightful smiles are rippling,
Her beautiful eyes are glancing,
Colours are painted on plain silk."*
What is the meaning of these three lines?

2

It means that when you paint, you have white as a base and then put colours on it.

3

It may mean that man must possess virtue first and then refine it with the practice of rites. Is that correct?

4

What you have said has enlightened me on the poem. It looks like I can only discuss The Odes with someone as bright as you are.

135

Tantai Mie Ming
澹台灭明

Tantai Mie Ming styled himself Zi Yu. He was a native of Wu Cheng and was younger than Confucius by thirty-nine years. Zi Yu, though ugly in looks, was an upright and honest man. In later years, he travelled to the states south of the Yangtzu River, where he recruited some three hundred students. He set up personal guidelines on give-and-take and observed them strictly. For this, his integrity spread widely among the lords.

1

Zi You was a steward of Wu Cheng.

2

Is there any virtuous man over there who can assist you?

3

There is this man called Tantai Mie Ming who does things according to the law and never takes short-cuts.

4

He never comes to my place except on official business.

Yuan Xian
原宪

Yuan Xian styled himself Zi Si and was a native of Lu. He was very poor and after the Master died, he went away to live by a remote river.

1

Hatred!

No. 1

WIN

When a man has gotten rid of such weaknesses as upmanship, conceit, hatred and greed, can we say he has achieved benevolence?

2

We can say that that is a rare man;

3

Whether he is benevolent or not, I'm not sure.

Zhuan Sun Shi
颛孙师

Zhuan Sun Shi, styled Zi Zhang, was a native of Chen and was younger than Confucius by forty-eight years. Zi Zhang was meticulous with attires and preoccupied with a stately presentation. For this reason, Zeng Zi once said of him: It is difficult to practise virtue in the company of a man like this.

1 Zi Zhang wanted to know how he could acquire an official post.

Listen widely to what people say to enrich yourself. Whatever you doubt, you can leave out but whatever you don't, repeat cautiously. In this way, there will be few mistakes.

2 Observe widely how people handle matters. What you don't feel right, don't do it,

but whatever you do, do it cautiously.

3 In this way, you will have few regrets and make few mistakes in your words and deeds. When that is achieved,

4 An official post will come your way.

138

Zeng Shen
曾参

Zeng Shen styled himself Zi Yu. He was a native of Nan Wu Cheng of Lu and was younger than Confucius by forty-six years. The Master felt he could understand filial piety thoroughly and so made him his pupil. Zeng Shen wrote a book entitled '*Xiao** Jing'. He died in his old age in Lu.

1

Shen, there is a thread that runs through my daily teaching of the Way.

2

Yes, Master.

3

What was the Master talking about?

4

The thread that the Master has mentioned is but made up of two words: **Loyalty** and **Forbearance.**

* *Xiao* means 'filial'.

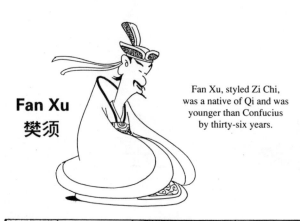

Fan Xu
樊须

Fan Xu, styled Zi Chi, was a native of Qi and was younger than Confucius by thirty-six years.

You Ruo
有若

You Ruo, styled Zi You, was a native of Lu and was younger than Confucius by forty-three years. After Confucius died, his pupils missed him badly and because You Ruo resembled the Master in appearance, they made him their teacher.

1. Harmony is utmost in the practice of the rites.

2. The ancient kings stressed the importance of harmony in whatever they did, be they small or big matters.

3. But that sometimes didn't work!

4. Just emphasising the beauty of harmony without the restraints of the rites will cause you problems.

*和 means 'harmony'   **礼 means 'rites'

141

Gong Ye Zhang

公冶长

Gong Ye Zhang, styled Zi Zhang,
was a native of Qi and
was Confucius' son-in-law.

1

This man Zi Zhang is good enough to be one's son-in-law. Although he was imprisoned, he was really not responsible for the crime.

2

And Confucius offered his daughter's hand to him in marriage.

Nan Gong Gua　南宫括

Nan Gong Gua, styled Zi Rong,
was a native of Lu.
Confucius had this to say about him:
"When the government was orderly,
he did not have to lose his office,
and when the government was
topsy-turvy, he managed to
keep clear of trouble."
And Confucius offered his brother's
daughter to him in marriage.

1. Yi excelled in archery, while Ao excelled in canoeing. Both were men of courage, but they died terrible deaths.

2. Xia Yu and Hou Ji were different. They took to ploughing the fields themselves and still ruled the world. Wasn't that true?

3. Since Confucius offered no answer, Zi Rong excused himself.

4. What a gentleman he is! What a follower of benevolence!

143

Gong Xi Chi
公西赤

Gong Xi Chi, styled Zi Hua, was a native of Lu and was younger than Confucius by forty-two years.

When Zi Hua went away on a diplomatic mission to Qi, Ran You applied to Confucius for household provisions on behalf of Zi Hua's mother.

Give him six bushels of grain.

Give him more, please.

Give him sixteen bushels then.

But Ran You took it upon himself to give him eight hundred bushels.

When Confucius knew about it, he said:

When Gong Xi Chi went away on a diplomatic mission to Qi, he was riding in a chariot drawn by well-fed horses and dressed in fine warm clothes. I have heard that a gentleman seeks to help others in need, not to increase his own fortunes.

Asiapac Comic Series (by Tsai Chih Chung)

Art of War
Translated by Leong Weng Kam
    The Art of War provides a compact set of principles essential for victory in battles; applicable to military strategists, in business and human relationships.

Book of Zen
Translated by Koh Kok Kiang
    Zen makes the art of spontaneous living the prime concern of the human being. Tsai depicts Zen with unfettered versatility; his illustrations spans a period of more than 2,000 years.

Da Xue
Translated by Mary Ng En Tzu
    The second book in the Four Books of the Confucian Classics. It sets forth the higher principles of moral science and advocates that the cultivation of the person be the first thing attended to in the process of the pacification of kingdoms.

Fantasies of the Six Dynasties
Translated by Jenny Lim
    Tsai Chih Chung has creatively illustrated and annotated 19 bizarre tales of human encounters with supernatural beings which were compiled during the Six Dyansties (AD 220-589).

Lun Yu
Translated by Mary Ng En Tzu
    A collection of the discourses of Confucius, his disciples and others on various topics. Several bits of choice sayings have been illustrated for readers in this book.

New Account of World Tales
Translated by Alan Chong
    These 120 selected anecdotes tell the stories of emperors, princes, high officials, generals, courtiers, urbane monks and lettered gentry of a turbulent time. They afford a stark and amoral insight into human behaviour in its full spectrum of virtues and frailties and glimpses of brilliant Chinese witticisms, too.

Origins of Zen
Translated by Koh Kok Kiang

Tsai in this book traces the origins and development of Zen in China with a light-hearted touch which is very much in keeping with the Zen spirit of absolute freedom and unbounded creativity.

Records of the Historian
Translated by Tang Nguok Kiong

Adapted from Records of the Historian, one of the greatest historical work China has produced, Tsai has illustrated the life and characteristics of the Four Lords of the Warring Strates.

Roots of Wisdom
Translated by Koh Kok Kiang

One of the gems of Chinese literature, whose advocacy of a steadfast nature and a life of simplicity, goodness, quiet joy and harmony with one's fellow beings and the world at large has great relevance in an age of rapid changes.

Sayings of Confucius
Translated by Goh Beng Choo

This book features the life of Confucius, selected sayings from The Analects and some of his more prominent pupils. It captures the warm relationship between the sage and his disciples, and offers food for thought for the modern readers.

Sayings of Han Fei Zi
Translated by Alan Chong

Tsai Chih Chung retold and interpreted the basic ideas of legalism, a classical political philosophy that advocates a draconian legal code, embodying a system of liberal reward and heavy penalty as the basis of government, in his unique style.

Sayings of Lao Zi
Translated by Koh Kok Kiang & Wong Lit Khiong

The thoughts of Lao Zi, the founder of Taoism, are presented here in a light-hearted manner. It features the selected sayings from Dao De Jing.

Sayings of Lao Zi Book 2
Translated by Koh Kok Kiang

In the second book, Tsai Chih Chung has tackled some of the more abstruse passages from the Dao De Jing which he has not included in the first volume of Sayings of Lao Zi.

Sayings of Lie Zi
Translated by Koh Kok Kiang

A famous Taoist sage whose sayings deals with universal themes such as the joy of living, reconciliation with death, the limitations of human knowledge, the role of chance events.

Sayings of Mencius
Translated by Mary Ng En Tzu

This book contains stories about the life of Mencius and various excerpts from "Mencius", one of the Four Books of the Confucian Classics, which contains the philosophy of Mencius.

Sayings of Zhuang Zi
Translated by Goh Beng Choo

Zhuang Zi's non-conformist and often humorous views of life have been creatively illustrated and simply presented by Tsai Chih Chung in this book.

Sayings of Zhuang Zi Book 2
Translated by Koh Kok Kiang

Zhuang Zi's book is valued for both its philosophical insights and as a work of great literary merit. Tsai's second book on Zhuang Zi shows maturity in his unique style.

Strange Tales of Liaozhai
Translated by Tang Nguok Kiong

In this book, Tsai Chih Chung has creatively illustrated 12 stories from the Strange Tales of Liaozhai, an outstanding Chinese classic written by Pu Songling in the early Qing Dynasty.

Zhong Yong
Translated by Mary Ng En Tzu

Zhong Yong, written by Zi Si, the grandson of Confucius, gives voice to the heart of the discipline of Confucius. Tsai has presented it in a most readable manner for the modern readers to explore with great delight.

《漫画中国哲学家系列》

仁者的叮咛

孔子说

编著：蔡志忠
翻译：吴明珠

亚太图书(新)有限公司出版
